What is washi tape?

Washi tape is a low-tack, decorative paper
tape that can (and should) be used on everything!
The word *washi* refers to the Japanese paper from which
the tape is made. Known simply as masking tape in Japan,
it can be layered for various effects, as most of it is slightly
transparent, and can be used to create large designs for
home décor or placed on a quick piece of correspondence for
an instant pop of color. While washi tape originated in Japan,
it is now made throughout the world.

What is in this kit?

- 2 rolls of coordinating, patterned washi tape

- 12 3″ (7.6 cm)-long wooden picks (for cupcakes)

- 4 6″ (15.2 cm)-long wooden picks (for cake toppers)

- 2 yards (1.8 m) of red and white twine

- 12 confetti bags

- One packet of multicolored confetti (to fill the individual bags)

How to use washi tape

TEARING OR CUTTING

Washi tape can be torn or cut. The deckled, irregular torn edge can add to the handmade look of a project. Cut the edges of the tape with scissors for a clean edge, use pinking shears for a zigzag edge, or tear the tape with a tape dispenser, for a tiny serrated edge.

To create shapes like small triangles, squares, or arrow-tipped ends use scissors to freehand cut the tape.

When making detailed shapes or trimming tape in place (for example, on a surface), use a dull craft knife to score the tape, then tear it away for a clean line.

CREATING PATTERNED SHEETS

To create patterned sheets, layer tape onto waxed paper, overlapping strips of tape slightly. Create a solid sheet of all one kind of tape or vary colors, widths, and patterns to create your own design.

Freehand cut shapes with
scissors, cut detailed shapes with a craft knife and
cutting mat, or punch shapes with craft punches. Use this
technique to make flags for your Cake Topper Bunting.

CREATING PLAIDS

Using washi tape to create plaids is a great way to start playing with color without pressure. Let go and experiment with the transparency of the tape and learn how solids create unique colors and patterns as they overlap. There are no rules for making fun and funky plaids. Create cards, postcards, or little framable works of art.

WRITING ON WASHI TAPE

Washi tape has a lightly waxy surface that will only take permanent inks. I prefer to use fine-point waterproof pens when adding messages or text. Allow the ink to dry a few moments before placing the tape on your project. Black and brown inks show up best, but experiment with various ink colors for different effects.

More fun with washi tape!

Here are some more fun ideas of ways to use washi tape.

CONFETTI POUCHES

Giant paper confetti turns any gathering into a party. Tuck handfuls of colorful confetti into little paper pouches bursting to be opened.

Instead of confetti, make little seed packets or glitter pouches.

CAKE TOPPER BUNTING

A miniature bunting looks oh-so-sweet atop a pretty cake. Using various colors and styles of washi tape, make a bunting with baker's twine or string tied to wooden skewers. Create multiples for various cakes so you have a collection for larger parties or events.

Use cake toppers year after year for a birthday tradition or create a new one every year for a birthday surprise!

CUPCAKE TOPPERS

Make cute cupcake toppers in a snap with a toothpick and washi tape. Use regular tape to create single- or double-point flags and skinny tape for miniature flags. Create coordinating sets for any occasion.

Add these little flags to pies, cookies, and other baked goods.

CELEBRATION BUNTINGS

Buntings are a cheerful addition to any space. Hang over a bed, window, or desk or place on a shelf to add a touch of whimsy. To create a traditional bunting with single-point flags, fold strips of washi tape over a string or ribbon, doubling the tape back onto itself. Place flags of various patterns and colors along the string, then cut each flag into a triangle shape and hang.

To create a bunting with double-point flags, add strips of tape in the same manner as the single-point flag bunting, and then cut a triangle away from the center of each flag, creating a double point.

Make a larger bunting of various shapes by mixing small single- and double-point flags with flags made from large strips of washi tape. Cut the large flags into scallops and other shapes. Layer patterns, colors, neons, and solids or add a message in tape with preprinted letters.

Because of the small scale of buntings, this a great project for the end of the roll when you only have a little tape left. You can also create large-scale buntings by placing washi tape on paper to create flags.

The author can be found on Instagram (#101washitape) and on Twitter (@ccerruti)

Design: Mattie S. Wells
Photography: Matthieu Brajot

ISBN: 978-1-63159-003-0

Printed in 2014
2 4 6 8 10 9 7 5 3 1
www.quartous.com